Ceremony, Healing, Mud & Fun

Lynn Gosney

To Jane and Faye
don't leave it
another two years

Love ya
Lynn

Published by Lynn Gosney
Copyright 2013 Lynn Gosney

All rights reserved.
No part of this publication may be reproduced, stored in a retrieval system, or transmitted in any form or by any means, electronic, mechanical, photocopy, recording or otherwise, without prior written permission of the copyright owners. Nor can it be circulated in any form of binding or cover other than that in which it is published and without similar condition including this condition being imposed on a subsequent purchaser.

ISBN: 978-1495995903

British Cataloguing Publication data:
A catalogue record of this book is available from the British Library

This book is also available as an ebook.

I dedicate this book to my dear parents for showing me how to love, care and share; my husband and my sons and their beautiful families for their constant support and love.

Contents

Acknowledgements 1
1: About the co-author 3
2: About Lynn Gosney.. 5
3: What the Ceremony Involves and Means 9
4: Reason for This Book 11
5: My First Calling 13
6: First Experience.. 15
7: Second Experience 19
8: Third Experience 21
9: Fourth Experience... 23
10: The People I Met and Their Influence 25
11: Michele's Lodges 27
12: Fifth Experience 29
13: My Journey and How I Changed.......................... 31
14: Sixth Experience... 33
15: The Calling of the Lodge – My First Solo
Experience... 37
16: The Journey Continues 41
17: Caer Corhrain 45
18: Respect and Honour... 49
19: The Mother's Song 57
20: People Who Have Helped Me on My Journey..... 61
21: Final Word.. 63

Acknowledgements

The Ancestors, who have guided me and walked by myside over the many years.

Mother Earth for the amazing sacred rocks from her belly.

The Standing people for the gift of the wood for the sacred fire and the bones of the lodge.

The Plant Spirits for their amazing healing properties.

Wendy Steel for bringing this book into being.

Peter Jones, Michele Claiborne, Andy Baggott, Eli, Pete Maxey, Bruce Scott, Lisa Rowe and Anne O'Connor.

Fire Keepers: Paul Johnson, Matt Rowe, Darren Smart, Lewis Skinner, Jane Austin, John Adams, Teena Cozens, and Lee Gosney-Hunt.

Not forgetting all the other friends who have helped out with fire over the years.

And last but not least the hundreds of people who have sat within the Sacred Sweatlodge.

1: About the co-author

My name is Wendy Steele and I am the author of Destiny of Angels – First book in the Lilith Trilogy and Wendy Woo's Year – A Pocketful of Smiles, 101 ideas for a happy year and a happy you. I also perform with ATS® dance group Tribal Unity.

After dancing with Touch the Earth at a particularly muddy but uplifting healing festival, Lynn and I started talking about her plans for a book. She was keen to share her knowledge of the sacred sweatlodge with others and had started writing down her experiences. I agreed to help.

Nine months later, the result is Ceremony, Healing, Mud and Fun – A Personal Journey of the Sacred Sweatlodge. I wrote some of the book from Lynn's notes and from our conversations together, but much remains in her own words for two reasons. For those of you that know her, I wanted you to hear Lynn speaking to you, but more than that, this is a personal journey and I was keen for you to feel that Lynn was sharing her experience directly with you.

2: About Lynn Gosney

My name is Linda Gosney, though everyone knows me as Lynn. I was born and raised in Britain and I am proud of my roots and heritage. For many years, I have been privileged to be able to facilitate the wonderful healing ceremony of the sacred sweatlodge.

I am a daughter, mother, granddaughter, mother-in-law, wife and friend. My calling is to serve.

I was born in Blackfen in Sidcup and moved to Maidstone when I first attended primary school. I was nurtured and loved by my parents who gave me the understanding of how to love and share. At school, I failed academically, rebelled and was threatened with expulsion. Though the school viewed me as the dunce to be sat in the corner with a hat on, the underlying reason for my behaviour was dyslexia.

As a child, I had imaginary friends and spent my happiest days in the garden in the earth, under the bushes with the fae folk and fairies. Once I turned thirteen, my mother insisted I forget my imaginary friends and be a normal teenager.

After leaving school, I began hairdressing. I was married at nineteen and had my eldest son at twenty. Two years later, my second son was born.

When divorce freed me from marriage, my true womanhood began. A spiritual path opened for me when I visited a psychic fayre and then joined a spiritualist movement where I sat in closed circle and worked as a medium on the rostrum for a couple of years.

I met and married my second husband, had my third son and then faced major health issues. Still as a member of a spiritual church, I underwent a series of major operations and experienced what I now know to have been a shamanic death, leading to rebirth. Also at that time I attended workshops at Stansted Hall, Arthur Findley College and found the drum. I was overwhelmed. The first time I held the drum I felt like I had when holding my children when they were just born. The drum indeed was a most precious gift as it opened me up. I then found the flute and with these two gifts came my voice.

I started to use mantra and sound which connected me to the spirit of the ancestors in a way that felt so natural to me, and from this introduction I began a remarkable time of self-healing and a change of path.

I could no longer work as a medium. I knew the existence of spirit but I felt drawn to empower people so that they could connect themselves and feel inwardly the same inspiration as the drum, flute and voice had awoken in me.

I stopped sitting in circle, stopped public mediumship and went full out to deepen my connection with all existence of spirit; I found my feet firmly planted on the Shamanic pathway.

Up to this point I had worked from a shed in my garden but then I moved to the bungalow next door to me where I started meditation groups, healing groups and awareness circles.

My journey had begun.

Now well traveled, I have seen some wonderful countries and met some amazing people. I have run workshops in Europe and the USA, and poured lodge in Washington State. But it's *my* homeland, where *my* heart is, and the tiny little island I love in Kent, that runs deeply in my veins.

I now spend my time running a Shamanic development centre on the Isle of Sheppey, helping people on their path. Our centre, Caer Corhrain, stands on the marshlands and is known by many as their Spiritual home. I have been married for 30 years and we have three sons, three daughters in law, who are like daughters to me, and seven wonderful grandchildren.

I am a musician, songwriter, flute player and lead vocalist in the tribal folk band, Touch the Earth. I am also a drum maker.

My work within the sweatlodge is one of healing and prayer. Over the years, I've come across many people who have had different and varied experiences within the lodge and these I want to share with you.

8

3: What the Ceremony Involves and Means

Guided by spirit, I run sweatlodges that encompass many traditions as well as our own. Some North American sweatlodges take on a structured, regimented form. They can be selective and rely on strict rules of etiquette. My lodges, 'Lynnie's Tradition', are less formal. Each lodge is approached with respect, honour, sound intent and integrity but they are safe and relaxed to promote healing.

I could validate myself by giving you the names of friends, as they are all great medicine people and I could validate myself further by giving you a name for myself that sounds really impressive like "Little Bird, She who Sings in the Tree Tops and Walks with Wolves" but would that make me or anyone with such an impressive name any better than those without one? Many of us do have spiritual names but they are kept for private use and for ceremony; they are not to be used to glorify the ego and impress the gullible.

I believe our own heritage and our own ceremonies are undervalued, thought not to be as colourful or as powerful as those of Native Americans, when in fact they are. I see no reason not to blend our own traditions with those of our native cousins, creating a 'world blend' suitable and relevant to all.

I run my lodge with guidance from Spirit. I have a strong connection with America and the Arizona desert. I love Native American traditions and ceremonies as they are so close to my own beliefs and I love the people too. Within my lodge I mix ingredients. We take many facets and the end result is an amazing blend.

The lodge is a commitment. It is a commitment to Spirit, the Ancestors, the Creator and to the people who enter. It is not a gimmick or a curiosity object. The lodge is a beautiful and safe place when treated with respect. It is the most moving and profound ceremony that can take you to the source and centre of the universe. The power of the prayers is immense and they manifest as they are spoken. This is why you should be cautious about what you ask for in lodge or the outcome may not come through as you imagine.

Working together during the day building the lodge, getting the rocks ready and placing intent builds up a powerful connection of healing and wholeness in the Earth Mother's womb. Coming together in song, chant and prayer affirms this deep connection. In the eternal dark, the waters turn to wash you and carry your prayers until you re-emerge, cleansed in mind body and spirit. You are re-born.

All new lodges are built with intent, ceremony and honour. Each of our lodge frames lasts between two and four years. For each lodge, natural materials are carefully sourced and appropriate offerings made.

Be sure you are truly comfortable before entering a lodge. Honour your inner self and your intuition, as you know what is best for you. A good way is going to a lodge on a recommendation, rather than in response to an advert you may have noticed. Attending the right lodge at the right time in your life is a wonderful experience, one that can change your life and show you the real magic of spirit.

4: Reason for This Book

Many years ago I was first introduced to this wonderful and powerful ceremony.

This was to be an amazing awakening on my life's journey. It has been one filled with beautiful people who have helped me and shaped me into the woman I am, with hard and testing times, many lessons, tears and lots of laughter. This is my personal story of how and what this sacred lodge has done for me, and the many people who have come and joined as one within the belly of the Earth Mother.

I now run a sacred sweatlodge on each of the eight Celtic festivals throughout the wheel of the year, connecting us to creation, to the seasons and to the cycles of life and death.

This is a story of how it all started. Join me on my journey as I take you back to the beginning, to the very first lodge I took part in. It is my intention that reading this will awaken something deep within you so that you too may find that this beautiful ceremony stirs something in your heart, as it did in mine.

12

5: My First Calling

When I first felt the call of the lodge, I was guided by spirit to seek out my teachers.

I've always had a connection with the Earth. As a young child my happiest times were spent under the bushes with my hands and feet in the earth. I loved the smell and often tasted it, much to my mother's despair, but this deep seated connection to the Earth was rekindled in my adult life and my need and desire to be closer to it grew.

I owe much to my friend Eli who, along with two other very dear friends, Michele and Andy, showed me the way. Initially I was confused – how could a non-native run a ceremony from a different culture? I started to look deeper, seeking the roots of the lodge and I found this ceremony took on different forms in different countries. It was not just a Native American ceremony but one performed across the world and this has been so throughout history. With this in mind, I set out on an amazing journey of discovery.

14

6: First Experience

Many years ago my circle of friends included a man who was interested in Native American people, their old ways of life, traditions and customs. I had heard about the sweatlodge. I wanted to find out more about it, what it was and what happened in it. The opportunity arrived one day when I was asked by this friend if I would like to take part in one. I had absolutely no idea of what was going to happen, but I was excited at the prospect of taking part.

The day arrived and the sun was shining and though early, the day was already hot. Armed with a towel, sarong and packed lunch, off I went. After driving for an hour, my mind lost in thought and my body coursing with nerves, we arrived in a field somewhere in Kent.

The first thing I saw was a round dome shaped structure next to a fire. There were some strange looking animal skulls by the entrance and an English man dressed like a Native American. Face to face with a group of strangers, I was starting to wish I had chosen retail therapy as my afternoon's enjoyment!

There were about seven other people there and they all introduced themselves. They were all friendly and one of the women led me to a tent to undress. The longer I was there the more I wanted out. They tried to reassure me that the heat was my friend and the dark of the lodge was nothing to worry about.

All of a sudden, there was a loud noise like a foghorn and we were all quickly marched towards the fire pit. The man who looked like an Indian beckoned me towards him, and proceeded to choke me with this foul smelling stuff that reminded me of Sunday roast chicken. Coughing and spluttering, I was told to enter the lodge.

Nervous and bemused I sat as, one by one, everyone entered. The man mumbled a few words to me about not panicking when the door was closed and to breathe through the heat. Down came the door and plunged the whole place into darkness. My heart was in my throat and I was sure that everyone could hear it beating against my chest. The man said something in a language I could not understand and then said in English that this would be a good hot lodge and he would see how much we could all take. That was it - I wanted out.

With panic beginning to rise, all I could think of was getting out and I called into the darkness, "Please let me out!"

"You'll be okay, wait and see," was the reply.

"No, let me out!" I cried again, as I clambered over the others to try to find the doorway.

Finally, the man dressed as a Native American called out to open the door and with utter relief I stumbled into the daylight. Shaking from head to toe and feeling highly embarrassed, I sat on the ground trying to pull myself together. Never again, I said to myself. The others echoed my words when hours later they came out of the lodge looking like roasted lobsters.

On returning home a few days later, I recounted my story to my friends, stating that never again would I take part in a sweatlodge. Little did I know then that many years later I would not only have taken part in many sweatlodges but would be privileged to run my own.

That day stirred something in me that I was unaware of until two years later.

7: Second Experience

My second sweatlodge: I had been working with a friend at the Mind, Body and Spirit festival in London and she invited me to go with her to a workshop, followed by a sweatlodge. I felt nervous but at the same time, I trusted this friend and felt reassured she would be with me.

The workshop was very pleasant and was run by a lady. She played the Native American flute beautifully. The morning went by quickly and before we knew it, it was time to enter the lodge. There must have been about eighteen people standing in a very cold wind waiting to enter. This lodge was much larger than the first one. We all went in and sat down. It wasn't as dark as my previous experience and I could make out the others as they took their seats. When the lady who was running the lodge asked for the rocks to be brought in, we got warm. Looking back now, I realise that this was a much better, more gentle introduction to the sweatlodge and nothing like my scary first experience. We sang and shared stories and though I didn't experience the heat, I enjoyed the time spent in there with everyone. The seeds of my future were starting to germinate within me.

20

8: Third Experience

My next encounter with a sweatlodge was a couple of years later. By this time, my friend and I had begun running drumming workshops. We were to run a Shamanic workshop at the Arthur Findley College at Stansted, Essex and we had arranged for a sweatlodge to be run during the course. My next experience was to be in a lodge facilitated by Wan-Nee-Chee. This time I didn't feel so nervous. We were told what was going to happen and how the ceremony would come together. I had a better understanding and was now more in tune with the concept of the ceremony.

Together, we all built the frame and covered the lodge. I was fascinated with the whole thing. I scrutinized Wan-Nee-Chee as he readied the lodge, watching everything he did. I saw how he placed tobacco in each hole in the ground that had been made for the poles of the frame to go into, and how he did everything with prayer and intent. I found myself asking him lots of questions, why do you do that and what is that for? A hunger was burning in me, raging with passion like the fire that was burning and heating the rocks, and I sought to learn all I could. When the time to lodge came, I was full of anticipation. I was excited and felt something stirring in my belly.

We had a beautiful lodge. Wan-Nee-Chee's wonderful voice rang in my ears, sending shivers down my spine with such beauty, intensity and powerful words; I sweated and said my prayers. My journey was starting. I felt drawn to this ceremony as though it was in my blood. It was an old ancestral awakening that was stirring in the depths of my very soul. I remember going to bed that night feeling different. Somehow I knew that my journey was taking me along a new road, one which was exciting and kind of scary all at the same time. I felt warm and calm and had a tingling all over my body, inside and out. It was as if my eyes had been polished and cleaned to help me see more clearly.

9: Fourth Experience

The next lodge I took part in was with my friend, in the countryside somewhere in Hertfordshire and I remember it vividly. We had gone there to take a one hour drumming workshop that was being run by someone my friend knew. I remember that lady had a guest there who played the Native American flute. This was to be another amazing discovery for me as it started me on my flute journey, another story in its own right.

We had a women's only lodge that evening which was a very laid back and somewhat disjointed affair. We didn't get hot let alone sweat, but being together in the dark and singing, chanting and sharing our experiences and our prayers was every bit as wonderful. I was rediscovering going back into the darkness of the womb, experiencing its stillness and beauty. We had a good lodge; it was how it was meant to be. I was looking forward to the next one but didn't know where or when it would be. I was like a little child waiting for the delights of Christmas. At least with Christmas you know it will be the same time in December as always but that wasn't enough for me. I wanted to lodge now but I had to wait.

What a long way I had come from my first terrifying experience three years previously and I knew this was where I needed to be. The lodge felt like second nature to me and I experienced an intense longing to get back to the earth, back into the dark and the heat. The calling was strong, really strong and although I wasn't Native American, I knew it was what I was supposed to be doing. The lodge is part of me,

23

who I really am and I knew my path would lead me further.

10: The People I Met and Their Influence

Edd Magee, Eagle Man, had been with us on the course we were running at the Arthur Findley College. Many people had experienced the sweatlodge with him and other teachers that we had arranged to come had shared their knowledge with us with many becoming my friends. I met my dear friends Michele Claiborne and Gerald St Clair at the college.

Michele ran the lodge at the college and showed my friend the way. Gerald was a flute teacher from New Mexico, who was instrumental in showing me the beauty of the flutes. He became a very good friend and I have spent time with him in his homeland.

It was while I was with him that I was privileged to be invited to a Navaho Elder's home. She was a charming Elder who invited us into her Hogan and cooked a simple meal for us. Outside in the burning desert sun, stood the structure that I had started to become so familiar with - the sacred sweatlodge. I was unable to take any photos of this at the request of her son, Marshall. However, I knew that one of my friends had already used my camera to take some shots of me, and in one of them I was standing by the lodge. Marshall asked me to promise that if any photos had been taken of the lodge that I would destroy them and this I did as soon as I got my film developed. I let no one see that photo. I didn't even ask him why; I just knew I needed to honour his request with no questions asked.

26

11: Michele's Lodges

At Michele's lodges we always had fun. She was a musician and her kindness mixed with her ancestry of both Native American and Celtic bloodline brought great knowledge and understanding to the ceremonies.

I remember one particular lodge when it was raining really, really heavily and we just couldn't get the fire to light. Much to the amusement of everyone there, James went indoors and came out with cooking oil and we put sunflower cooking oil all over the fire to ignite it...and it worked!

Another time, because Michele's fire was quite close to her lodge, when everyone was inside drumming, singing and dancing, we suddenly realised that the actual lodge was on fire! There was plenty of laughter that night.

Once, when Michele had just come back from India, it was winter and freezing cold so she decided that we all needed to be smudged in the house in the warm. We proceeded to be smudged and cleansed by the sacred sage in the kitchen, and couldn't believe it when we saw she was boiling up the kettle to heat the water in the bucket that was to be put on the rocks, because she didn't want to put her hands in the cold water. All because she had just come back from warmer climates! None of this detracted from the power of the lodge as our intent and focus were unchanged.

So as the years unfolded, we did many lodges at Michele's house until there was a time when she no longer poured lodge. She moved on and though by this time, I had become established with the pouring of lodges at Trosley, I hoped that one day we would sit in lodge together again as we had shared some really special experiences.

12: Fifth Experience

After about a year, we began planning another workshop at The Arthur Findley College. Once again, a sweat was planned and it was to be my friend's first lodge as a facilitator. It was to be held at night and was to be women only. This was a good lodge and a hot one. It started a lot later than we had planned and I was getting very unfocused in the lodge, as I knew that the hour was getting very late, or I should say early. I had to drive back home from Stansted to be at work by 8.30am. This was because the day of the lodge had been postponed and, wanting to be in the lodge, I thought I would have plenty of time to lodge and get home in time for work. This was a big lesson for me.

A few of the new girls who had not lodged before left the rounds before the end of the lodge. They had gone out, got dressed and taken their belongings back to the college building. In my panic about time, I told my friend that I needed to leave. When I got outside it was total darkness. I had no torch and I looked everywhere for my bag of clothes but they were nowhere to be found. I was panicking and must have looked really funny running around like a mad naked woman, with just a towel to keep me from freezing in the cold night air. I made it back to the college from the grounds without being seen - I think! I rested for an hour and then drove home, tired and tearful, thinking I never wanted to do any more of those mad things in the dark late at night ever again.

This lodge was to be the end of the special working relationship I had with my friend, and we went our separate ways not long afterwards.

The college just didn't seem to understand Shamanism. They were not sympathetic to our way of teaching and conflict was not something I wanted. I had seen many people set out their outdoor altars with love and passion. They felt the love of the spirits of the land and those special places. They worked hard to put the lodge frame up and to create the sacred circle that was formed, only to be told afterwards that they couldn't use it and that they had to break it all up. This came as a heavy blow to us. We'd had good times together and met good people but without the understanding of the college, our work there could not continue.

13: My Journey and How I Changed

For what seemed like a long time my sweatlodge path appeared to take a back seat. Not in my heart but I just didn't know where to go to find one. It was a time of change for me, as I was becoming less interested in the Native American way of life. My own ancestral heritage was calling me and I wanted to know more about my own homeland, ceremonies and rituals.

Everywhere I went people wanted to talk Native American. They wanted to dress like them and take part in their sun dance and pipe ceremonies. Beautiful as the ceremonies and people are, I felt we should know about our own background and our own ceremonies and not take blindly from others. I felt a hunger gnawing at me. I was unsure exactly what I felt at the time but now I understand that it was my eagerness to find out more about this wonderful ceremony of the sweatlodge that had entered my life and without which my life now seemed so strange. Where to go now? I didn't have a clue. I just said my prayers to the universe and waited, for I knew that if something was meant to happen it would and that it would unfold in my life. Unfold it did, in a most amazing way.

32

14: Sixth Experience

For a number of years I had been running a healing centre in Gillingham, Kent where I lived with my husband and three sons. I ran meditation groups, spiritual development groups and we had a team of dedicated healers who offered their time freely every Thursday evening. The centre had grown and had become well known and popular.

A man called Simon contacted me and asked if he could come to my meeting one night. He came along and ended up staying with me for a good few months and we became good friends. He was a supply teacher and was working in the area so he needed a place to live for a while.

One evening we sat talking and he told me of a friend of his that lived in Somerset. He said that his friend had a nice place down there and that he ran sweatlodges. I felt a surge of excitement overwhelm me at the mere thought of having an opportunity of at last finding another sweatlodge. In the weeks that followed, arrangements were put together and one Saturday in summer, a group of us headed for Somerset. This day's outing heralded a chain of events that changed my life forever.

We left early for the trip to Somerset, which was to become a journey that I have made many times now and still make today. All the way there I was full of excitement. We arrived at lunch time to find the house in a village tucked away from the road side.

As we entered we met Andy who, straight away, made us all feel at home. He was tall with long hair tied back in a ponytail. He showed us where to make our tea, as often as we wanted. Then a beautiful woman entered the kitchen. Silent in her beauty, she swept in and smiled at us with such warmth that I felt something straight away with her - a connection that was new but also old.

It was a very hot summer's day so we all sat in the garden for a while until Andy said it was time to cover the lodge. Together we helped put the covers over the small round hazel frame that stood under the tree in the garden. Next to the lodge there was a fire pit and a large pile of freshly cut wood waiting for the fire. Then Andy told us how to choose our rocks that would be placed on the fire pit. We each picked a rock and said a prayer to the creator and to Mother Earth before facing each direction and saying another prayer. Then we placed the rock onto the fire. We put a pinch of salt and tobacco on the rocks. I asked Andy why and he told me salt was sacred to our Celtic ancestors as was tobacco to our Native American brothers.

The fire was then lit by a man who fascinated me. He wore colourful shorts along with boots and no shirt. His name, I was later to learn, was Eli and he was the fire keeper of the lodge.

We all gathered for the lighting of the fire while Andy drummed and chanted a song with words I had never heard before, and the fire took hold straight away so that soon the flames were dancing. We sat around the fire and played drums while the men played the didgeridoo. It was a beautiful day.

The time came when we were told the rocks were calling and we got ourselves ready for the lodge. This was to be the most amazing experience of my life other than when I gave birth to my three beautiful sons. The darkness, the closeness, the prayers, the chants and songs filled my senses and fed my spirit. This was where I belonged. I had come home. After this day, my life was never going to be the same again.

36

15: The Calling of the Lodge – My First Solo Experience

The next day I was invited to join Eli in the woods where he was living. It was beautiful woodland, deep, dense, very ancient and welcoming. He showed me his simple Bender home and took us around the woods. We became friends. Whilst walking with Eli and Andy I told them of my feelings and that the lodge was calling to me but I wasn't sure if I should be running them.

Andy pulled me up sharply. "Nothing can stop you only yourself. It's all about intent and honesty. If you are meant to run a lodge then it will be so."

A few months later, with my friend Teena and another friend, we went to camp with Eli in the woods. It was to be a very good lesson in how to run a sacred sweatlodge. We set up our tent and it was cold, very cold. We got a fire going and darkness fell. Eli had helped us to carry all our many belongings to where we set up our tent. Uphill, trip after trip we made, carrying all the items we had with us. We had never stopped to think about keeping it simple and we had everything with us, including the kitchen sink! Eli just smiled at us and loaded another wheelbarrow. We had brought a couple of large bottles of water as we knew there was no tap where we were camped out. Never before had I realised how heavy water was until we had to fetch more within hours of being there, having used it all with cups of tea, washing-up and sheer waste. This was Lesson one. Lesson two was digging a hole when we went to the loo!

The next day Eli told us we would lodge that night so the four of us entered another adventure. Lesson three began. He led us over three fields, full of cows, and into a wood where we selected some hazel poles. He showed us how to ask the tree permission before we took them and how we should give an offering in return. When we had enough poles, we had to carry them all the way back over the three fields, through the mud with the cold wind biting our faces.

When we got back, he showed us how to build the lodge and how to cover it with canvas. As we pulled the canvas up we discovered that there was something dead and smelling on it. Teena and I tried not to gag at the smell and we began to understand that if you lived out in the wild, then this was all part of the experience. All was done with intent and offerings. Teena and I sat down, feeling pleased with ourselves but Eli shook his head.

Lesson four began. Eli took us over the fields again and down into the quarry to get the rocks. We lost count of how many times we did this until Eli said there should be enough. We collapsed wearily to the ground and stayed there until Eli rallied us once more and we set off gathering wood for the fire. He showed us how to build the fire which covers the rocks. The fire was lit; we sang around it and held ceremony as the darkness of night crept in. There was an air of anticipation among us and a feeling of magic. So dark was the wood, we could hear the owl hooting his night call, the stars pierced the night sky and the air was crisp and cool. Then it was time for us three women and Eli to enter the lodge.

Eli poured the water on the rocks and took the first round and it was wonderful. The second round came and he went out to bring in more rocks He then said to me, "I leave the rest of this lodge to you". Oh boy! Panic or what!

Lesson five: Learning to trust. I sat, calmed down and tuned into the energy of the lodge. I asked for help and guidance and it was given. We had another two rounds, just us three women, and it was beautiful. I had just taken my first lodge.

40

16: The Journey Continues

Over the course of a year, I met with Eli in the woods and he shared a great deal of his knowledge with me.

To this day, I honour and respect the teaching this wonderful man gave me and I am thankful to him for the path he opened to me. I will never forget the wise words he gave me on that day "you put Jack Shit in, you get Jack Shit out!" such truth in these words.

I spent time with Andy and Debbs and worked very hard on my own self-healing, deep stuff which also helped to make and shape me into who I am today.

As time went by, I started to look for a place local to my home where I could build lodge and give others the opportunity to experience this amazing ceremony. I met Rob Wilson, who walked the path of Druidry, and together we embarked on a mission to find somewhere for a lodge. We put out our prayers and intent and came upon a possible site. It was ancient woodland near to where Rob lived - Trosley Country Park. We got to know the ranger and all was set. We would make a donation to the park for every lodge we had.

Trosley wasn't an ideal location, being a public park, but we knew it was another step on the journey and we had some interesting lodges there.

On one occasion we were all standing around the fire pit in ceremony when a host of marathon runners, all sporting large black numbers on their backs, came running past. Another time, though the met office had issued weather warnings to stay indoors, we held lodge in a gale and couldn't hear the person sitting next to us. As we often camped out after lodge, I remember cooking soup for everyone bare footed and ankle deep in mud!

At another lodge in Trosley Woods a lady visited us and felt compelled to take part. She took her husband's t-shirt off his back to wear in place of a sarong, sent him home and entered her first lodge. Lisa still regularly lodges with us and her husband, Matt, is one of our dedicated fire keepers.

While at Trosely Woods we were still travelling long distances for our lodge rocks. It was a mammoth job, a long drive and very hard work. In a quest to find rocks nearer to us, we ended up with a friend visiting a stone site in Sussex and finding one rock the size of a sheep. We fell in love with it. Gary, our friend could hardly believe it when Rob and I said this was the one we wanted but, true to his word, Gary helped us. The rock was crane lifted onto his small lorry which struggled to our home under the weight. The day was cold and the land covered in fine snow but bright with sunshine as we carried home our rock of Norwegian granite, shining and sparkling like a jewel. We needed to break it up into smaller pieces for lodge so Gary took it to work with him. Being a builder, he tried a kango, but it broke twice trying to crack the rock. He resorted to dropping it a few times from a JCB and we were rewarded with rocks for our lodge. They heated beautifully and the rocks too large for lodge still stand today in our stone circle and are honoured for their strength and beauty.

One day we arrived at Trosley Woods to run a lodge to find someone had laid flowers in the pit, which was both a beautiful and moving sight. While always carried out with integrity, laughter has also been a part of lodge. On one occasion a lady emerged into the dark from the lodge and was adamant her welly boots had been taken, only to find her feet had swollen in the heat and would no longer fit into her boots!

When we left the woods, my ever helpful and amazing husband transported our lodge frame on our rascal van. It looked so funny, as if we were taking home a very large spider.

Wonderful times that I shall always remember were had in those lodges in the woods.

44

17: Caer Corhrain

Many times I would ask that if it was for the highest good of all, that we would be blessed with a place where we could hold our lodges and workshops. I envisioned a place where people could come to get away from the built up towns and where they could connect with the spirit of the land. We wanted a place with room to camp out, to have fire ceremonies, feel the abundance of nature and see the beauty of our native wildlife. This dream was my intent and it manifested in my life as Caer Corhrain.

The site was amazing and as soon as we saw it everything fell into place. The very day I first viewed it, I pulled three cards out with the numbers 8, 10, and 12. I just knew that we would sign on the 8th month, move in on the 10th month and be settled by the 12th month. How accurate that all was! Our date for moving in was the 31st of October, the Celtic New Year, and what a year that was to be.

The marshlands have brought inspiration to many. Beautiful songs have been written, wonderful healing sweatlodges have taken place, our Maypole has been danced with joy and a summer solstice camp enjoyed by many. This place is surrounded by poplar trees and willow. Barn owls live in the barn along with bats flying at dusk. The hare runs with the speed of light across the fields and dragonflies dance in the sunlight. The heron and many other feathered friends are constant visitors, along with rabbits, ducks and the fox. Lying in direct view of Minster Abbey on the horizon, the place is peaceful and has an amazing energy.

After a wonderful sweatlodge with my very dear friend, Andy Baggott, I had a vision of a new sacred space where we could all work together. After putting my trust in Spirit, and indeed with the support of my husband and a few very dear friends, a beautiful log cabin was erected in our meadow overlooking the fields. My vision and trust in spirit has been repaid through the many wonderful workshops that have since been held there.

The name of this amazing place was born in a lodge. Rob was given the name Caer Corhrain. Many have passed through and felt the magic of the land, the stillness and love that embrace us every day and night. It is a place born out of love of spirit and the sacred land, my home, your home and home to many who are ready to feel its embrace.

We settled in at Caer Corhrain and started to run our lodges. It was hard in the early days because although we live on a little island very close to the mainland, with just a little bridge, nobody wanted to deliver wood over here. It is a strange life on this little Isle of Sheppey, one that I really love but you would think it was Timbuktu! With no wood delivery, Rob and I used to go out in my little Rascal van, load it with wood and come back and unload it. Nothing was easy to begin with but this is one of the things I like about the journey of the sweatlodge. It isn't easy. It's hard work. It is blood, sweat and tears. We go down and get the rocks from the belly of the Earth and bring them back here, and we go to the hazel woods to coppice the hazel poles. There are, however, benefits to Caer Corhrain. We don't have to carry the water very far as we have an outside tap and it's easy to get the coverings out of a special shed I have now, instead of having to wheelbarrow them from the car park. So, in a way the lodges here are absolute luxury and people really don't realise just how luxurious they have it here and how easy it actually is.

I always feel a little bit surprised, no surprised is not the right word... I always find it quite amusing, should I say, that I have people come for their first lodge and they say "Wow! This is fantastic!" and then they want to do it themselves. We all have to start somewhere of course, and there was a time when I didn't have a clue, but I have got to where I am through hard graft. I have got to where I am through working with spirit, being guided and listening. Time and experience are important. Learning from good teachers is essential. From those early days, it's important for me to honour my teachers like Michele, Andy and Eli, who were instrumental in the start of my journey and have led me to where I am today.

48

18: Respect and Honour

Over the years I have seen so much disrespect by people and their attitudes, even over sourcing the rocks. I have taken a long time to source my rocks and it was a dear friend who shared their source with me. I hold on to that dearly because I don't want this place plundered or disrespected. If people are meant to find their own lodge rocks then they will, like I have. Caer Corhrain has two sources. We don't go out and buy them from the quarries and we don't expect them to be delivered to our doorstep. We go out, we quest the places and we tune ourselves in to these places. We honour the spirits of those places and Mother Earth for spilling forth the beautiful rocks. We carry each rock individually and, believe me they are heavy, and bring them back in cars. I only take a few trusted friends with me to do that.

I have had some very interesting conversations with people who have done one lodge and think it's easy and want to set themselves up a sweatlodge. There is so much more to it than that! Integrity and respect are vital and so many people who have approached me have neither. One day, as I arrived at work, first thing in the morning, I received a text. 'Where do you get your sweatlodge rocks from?' it read. I'd believed the sender had a better knowledge of honouring and respect but there was none for me or for Mother Earth so there was no way I would divulge such precious knowledge to someone like that in reply to a question that was so casually asked.

I have had many people look at the lodge and say, "Oh yeah, I can do this. I can build this. I want a lodge in my garden." Why do you want a lodge in your garden? What's your intent? What's your reason? Is it just to go along with all the other things you are doing? Lodge is a calling. It's a dedication and when the people come to lodge they process feelings and experiences and even after they have gone you have to be there ready to help them through if they need it. The lodge is a catalyst for healing, mega healing. You have to be there and be willing to help and see people through those doorways. It is not just the physical things or just a place to hold lodge or resource the materials. It is a big, big picture.

The lodge is sacred and I get very concerned sometimes when I see people frivolously thinking they can run a lodge when they have no experience or understanding of what it really means. I know that if you are meant to run a lodge Spirit will direct you and their hands will guide you all the way. But there are so many people out there on ego trips, so trust your intuition. If you decide to go into a sweatlodge go with someone who has come to you from a recommendation or someone that you know and you trust. I have had people enquiring about my sweatlodge saying "The last one I went to was a certain price per hour, how much do you charge a round?" Setting a price per hour or per round undermines the integrity of the ceremony and those who do so show nothing but disrespect by what they are doing.

I have had people come to me who have had distressing experiences in lodges, like my own first experience, because they weren't held in the correct way and they've emerged unbalanced and frightened. It certainly hasn't helped with their healing and a lot of damage has been done. It has taken me a long time to actually help these people and get them back to trusting again.

I don't normally facilitate lodges anywhere but Caer Corhrain, Norfolk or Bear Creek in Washington State. I've been asked to facilitate at festivals but always decline. Part of the lodge is the preparation, not only to physically prepare the ceremony but also to have time for people to build a bond, a spiritual connection before they take part. The intent of those joining together to enter the lodge can only be ascertained over the day so this, and the vital follow on support for lodgers, makes properly facilitating lodge at festivals not possible.

We have had many people who have come here and gone through our lodge. I like that the lodge is tuned to the 8 Celtic festivals so we don't just use an East door, but a West, South and North one as well. We use the different doors to change the flow depending on the season we are celebrating. We have had many lodges in different weather conditions, all unique to the place of the wheel we are celebrating. The weather never stops us holding lodge. It's so very beautiful when it snows but it can bring its own challenges. It isn't for the faint hearted as the bitter cold can hurt your feet as you wait to enter the lodge but there is nothing more amazing than coming out of the lodge with steam coming off your body and witnessing a dark star studded sky. We've emerged from lodge to pouring rain washing the heat off us or cool crisp white snow to roll in.

One year, when the snow was really heavy, in our excitement we rushed to cover the lodge and it was not until we entered that night in the dark we realised we had forgotten to clear the snow from inside the lodge first! Oh my goodness it was cold on your arse, even the water in the bucket froze at the top from time to time despite the heat of the lodge. However, the beauty of this lodge was coming out streaming hot and lying in the snow. It was exhilarating and it looked so funny as people moved and the beautiful moon was shining bright and showed the shapes of peoples body's where they had melted the snow, looked like rows of gingerbread people. Nevertheless, I never made the mistake of failing to clear the snow out before lodging again! It wasn't the first time I had to break the ice in my bucket or we had to battle high winds and rain. In the woods we had to take care in the heat of the summer and be mindful of the fire, here at Caer Corhrain we have to be mindful of the grass and fields of wheat which we are surrounded by. But these are all the elements we work with and who we acknowledge with honour and respect.

We hold lodges in any weather condition and for many reasons

On one occasion, we had an all-night Solstice lodge; we entered at sunset and came out at sunrise WOW!! and infused with our prayers were drum hides which we were to create the next day into Pow Wow's and hand drums, sacred drums honoured in lodge.....a wonderful experience. One lodge we had in the woods we had the most amazing storm, on the news and radio we were told to expect high winds and that people should only go out if they really needed to, well! We had lodge, sitting in there within the wind and rain was amazing, the wind was so loud you could not hear the people in lodge speaking, it was wild! My poor old mum was quite distressed when she saw me afterwards her words to me were "everyone was home safe, not you, not my daughter, only you could be up the bloody woods in the dark in a raging storm" Bless her. "Mum" I said "we were safe, no trees came down and no one was hurt we were in ceremony all was safe and well". She never really could understand.

We have what we call 'open lodges' and what we call 'closed lodges'. 'Open lodges' are where I will bring new people in with experienced lodgers so they can share the experience, while 'closed lodges' are only for experienced lodgers. I have always found that having experienced lodgers in with people who haven't lodged before works well. It eases them in, gives them somebody to talk to during the day and someone to answer their questions. Believe me, when anyone comes for their first lodge and says they are not frightened and they are not apprehensive, I know that the lodge will soon humble them.

We've had people come to lodge in high heel shoes, 'dressed to the nines' in fancy clothes, asking me questions like 'Have you sweated with real Indians?' The lodge will quickly humble those with large egos. On the other hand one nervous lodger was instrumental in manifesting his greatest fear, a rock dropping on him. It had never happened before but this time a rock fell and just missed him illustrating that the lodge has ways of showing you so much.

Having experienced lodger's present with new lodgers proved invaluable when a man without honour took part in our lodge one night. Our experienced lodger stopped his misdemeanours by calling out in the darkness, 'My god! There's a bloody great rat trying to nibble my toe!' Needless to say, the newcomer never entered our lodge again. In lodge or outside it is truly magical and the energy is not something one can easily explain. One lodge I was told by the spirits to leave on the third round, I didn't question it, when I am that "hollow bone" I open myself to the spirits and serve. I left lodge to stand by the fire and gave the antlers over to Jon, who I had been showing the way to. Next thing I know was being guided by the spirits to take in the other last remaining rocks. Nothing strange in that you may think! Only that all I was wearing was rubber flip flops and a very muddy wet sarong. I don't recall it that well as they were still working through Me, but was told afterwards that my fire keepers and my son stood there with their mouths wide open in sheer disbelief! If you have ever witnessed a lodge fire you will fully understand. When tending fire it's very hot, very wild and you dance with its spirit, you need no fear and to trust it. You must honour it or it will kick your arse for sure. When tending fire you wear gloves, hat and protective clothes as you need to get right into the fire to retrieve the rocks. Not only did I enter with so little on I was given the strength to almost run with the rocks on the fork to deliver them to those waiting, with a bad back it's no easy task under normal conditions. It's a story that we often reflect on with disbelief, when there's a strong connection and trust in Spirit it's easy to serve to help others experience the wonders of this sacred ceremony.

It can be hard work and the fire keepers need to keep in touch with the spirits of the fire at all times. One particularly windy Imbolc, the fire keepers had to lie on the lodge to keep the covers on it. It is indeed an honour to work the fire, I love it, it's hot and very hard work in some cases you could be tending that fire for

10 or 12 hours. Just recently I been honoured to keep fire here at Caer Corhrain and in October 2013 I kept fire up at our sister community in Bear Creek Washington State USA with Darren. It was a great honour to keep fire for our dear friend and wonderful Elder and medicine teacher Patrick Pinson and his community. We worked that fire for ten hours. The weather was still and fresh that day and the moon bright and shining over the tall cedars high on the mountains. Each lodge and each fire is different and is unique. The power of the fire is evident when you look at the front cover of this book. The Fire was one of our Ancestral lodges held at Samhain, Old soul's night. The mighty fire stag showed us his presence. Stag is one of my power allies that comes to me when I need courage to push through something and stand strong. He came to us that night and blessed our fire and helped us with a situation that was going on and is always there as a reminder to us of the power of lodge fire and the path we walk.

19: The Mother's Song

Each lodge at Caer Corhrain is special and unique. The healing, connection and oneness we feel is hard to put into words. Taking part is the only way to truly understand the experience. We have had Elders within our lodge to share their teachings and we have had an army of ants that share a deep and profound lesson. The youngest lodger was 5 weeks old inside his mother's womb and we've lodged young men and women completing their rites of passage, and women having crone celebrations.

People experience profound changes in their lives after a lodge. It is truly one of the most powerful and empowering ceremonies there is. Each lodge, as I've said, is different but I never tire of hearing people sharing, laughing, crying and healing and listening to their heartfelt prayers.

I called a closed family lodge when each of my parents crossed to the Summerlands. We had 53 rocks for my mother and 56 for my father, a rock for each year of my life they had given to me. The lodge is a wonderful, magical place to be when you are in pain at such times. The Sacred lodge and the entering into the womb of Mother Earth will help you re-balance; it's truly a place where you are free to be yourself

The doors are low so we may humble ourselves before the Creator and all spirit.

This is a song I wrote that we sing in lodge and it's what the lodge is all about:

Song to the Mother

Oh mother we sing to you
Deep deep in your womb
Oh mother we come to you

Deep deep in your womb
Deep in your belly
We honour you
Oh mother of all

A way anhaner
Way anhnanra
A way away a ho

Oh mother we pray to you
Deep deep in your womb
We honour all women
We honour you
Oh mother of all

A way anhaner
Way anhnanra
A way away a ho (repeat)

Our blessed blood
Flows into earth
The womb the mother's call
Sacred womb, sacred womb
Holds the seeds of life

The commitment to lodge is one I stand by. We often hear excuses from people about why they have dropped out, and that's fine but I believe that if they did take part, they would understand the power of truth.

From hot sunshine to deep snow to high winds and heavy rain, we lodge, although of late, the high winds and rain have been a challenge to us. However it's amazing to see people standing in rain, biting cold winds and snow, waiting to enter the lodge, so strong is their resolve to take part in this amazing ceremony.

The last year (2012) has been wetter than I can ever remember. Our lodge stands on marshlands with a high water table so, not only do we lodge in wet and cold, but in ankle deep mud too. Our fire pit has sat in water and our pit in lodge has become a hot spring when rocks are placed within it. And then there's the mud, oozing between our toes, hanging from our bodies and caked in our hair. The ground has been so slippery in parts that if you stand in one place, you sink but what wonderfully high and healing prayers have been experienced in the lodges we have had. Three showers are needed to get the mud from your body but what a feeling it is to have truly been part of the Earth.

At this point I must mention two people, Bruce and Pete. I have never felt drawn to show this way to anyone else. Pete and Bruce just sat by my side, as they do with the music, and they learned. Recently I have met people and guided by messages in lodge, I have asked them if they would like to walk the wheel with me for three years and I will share with them all my knowledge of pouring a lodge. I am not getting any younger and I realise that the gift I have been given needs to continue on when I am just dust. I want to share this beauty with many so they too can experience it and I now have people who I know can take this ceremony, share it with respect, with integrity, with intent, with honour and in truth. How blessed am I to have these people to share this with. May the lodge continue to bring healing, connection and balance to all those that enter. It is with heartfelt gratitude and vast abundance that I say thank you to all who have helped make my journey with lodge possible. A Hey Nama Te!

If the lodge does call to you, make sure you feel comfortable with the person who is pouring the lodge. Make it your business to find out. You are going into an incredibly sacred ceremony and it is very, very powerful. It is not a gimmick. It is a very, very powerful ceremony. Ceremony, healing, mud and fun.....I hope you feel the call.

20: People Who Have Helped Me on My Journey

So many people have helped with the lodge over the years. I honour all those who have helped bring the lodge together. It truly is an amazing experience. It is exciting and moves you in ways you would never believe. We get down in the Earth. We get cold and we get wet. We get mud between our toes, under our fingernails and toenails and we get mud, grass and leaves in our hair. We smell the fragrance of Mother Earth and feel her heart beating and connecting to ours. The steam cleanses us, washes away the fears, washes away the pain, releases that spirit within us, helps us to be in the self, to sit comfortably in the darkness and go within the self. It allows us to heal, to rebalance and to reconnect to all that is

The lodge is pure magic. It is one of the most powerful, healing and honouring ceremonies that one could ever take part in. I give thanks to the spirits and those who have guided me to be able to facilitate this ceremony for so many people over the years. May I ask that I continue to do so for all the time my bones allow me to bend to get into the lodge, where I humble myself before the creator, honouring Mother Earth, to lie down in the womb on the ground and to hold the energy. May I continue to do so for many years to come.

Paul is one of our amazing fire-keepers who brought his energy to our ceremony, showing others how to hold fire in a sacred way. When my friend Teena moved away to the Midlands, I put out my request for a really good fire-keeper and that's when Paul came on to the scene. Being American he had poured many lodges out there, keeping fire for some wonderful medicine teachers. His way is the way we have taken on here as it is one of honour and respect. The fire pit and the fire are held sacred. We do not put any rubbish on our fire at all. It is all good wood and every piece of wood is handled with love and respect, honouring the sacrifice it is making by going onto the fire.

Paul passed on his knowledge to Matt, Jane and Darren. As they work it's like watching true artists. I always say to people when we gather and we are getting ready to bless our rocks around the fire before it is lit, to look after the fire-keepers because their part is more important than mine. Without good fire-keepers the rocks don't heat and can't release their wisdom and the lodge doesn't work. I have the utmost respect for those who keep fire. I have kept fire myself and believe me when I say it is incredibly hard work. You get singed hair, singed eyebrows, singed skin and Matt has set his trousers alight many a time but, it is always accepted with humour, respect and much honour.

21: Final Word

I give thanks first and foremost to the Ancestors that guided me on this amazing sacred sweatlodge journey and for the many sharers of the knowledge along my way of learning.

Thank you Teena for all our madness in those early days. The fun and frolics, when we used to camp at Cranmore Woods with our trusty shovel.

Thank you to Andy and Debbie Baggott, Michele Claiborne and to those who I met in those early days who set me on this amazing path. Thank you to Eli for making the path of the sweatlodge possible for me and for your guidance in the early days. Thank you to my dear friend, Michele. You really showed me the way of lodge and how to hold that energy in a gentle, loving way.

I would like to thank my Mum and Dad because it was their abundance of love, of loving me, of loving everyone that gave me that gift, so that I am able to love and share. I honour them for leading me onto this beautiful path.

I remember that I had always wanted some antlers and had been questing for some for a long time to help me bring the hot rocks into the lodge. We had been on holiday in the New Forest and went to a place called Burley where, in a witches shop, there were antlers hanging everywhere, perfect for what I wanted. I looked at the price and having young children I just couldn't afford them.

My Dad looked at me, "Do you want them?" he said.

"Yeah, I do," I said.

"Well, if you want them, you have them," he said.

The shop assistant got them down and he looked at them. "I don't know what my daughter wants them for," he said, "But I love her and I will buy them for her". That was my Dad and he is always with us in lodge with those antlers.

Thank you to Patrick Pinson of Cedar Mountain Drums, Portland, Oregon, USA for inviting me to his lands to bring our Celtic lodge to his community at Bear Creek, Carson, Washington.

Thank you to the many rock people who came to us and have shared their healing and wisdom and to the many standing people whose limbs created our womb and heated our fires.

Thank you to the Spirits of Fire, Water, Air and Earth that blended their energies to bring the sacred lodge.

A heartfelt thanks to all the many dedicated fires keepers over the years, for without their hard work in all conditions the lodges would not have been.

I'm very lucky to have a very reliable man who brings wood over every six to eight weeks to Caer Corhrain in his lorry, so I no longer have to go and get the wood, load it in my car and then unload it again. I honour him.

To all the hundreds of people over the years that sat in lodge with me, who put their trust in my hands. It was an honour to share with you all.

To my family for their love and support over the years when on occasions, the lodge has taken priority over everything else.

Thank you to my husband, who has always supported us, never entered a lodge but understands its importance to me and the community and for his practical skills, ensuring a well-tended lawn and looking the other way when it's been churned up by lots of muddy feet.

To Bruce Scott and Pete Maxey who pour the lodge with the same love, truth, honour, respect, intent and integrity as I. It's been a privilege to share the knowledge of lodge with you all.

And last but not least to the amazing Wendy Steele for bringing this book into reality for nothing but kindness and a wish to share my story.

To the lodge and all who have sat and will sit within I say thank you.

"In truth, honour, respect, intent and integrity always."

Lynn xx (Linda Anne Gosney)

Made in the USA
Charleston, SC
16 March 2014